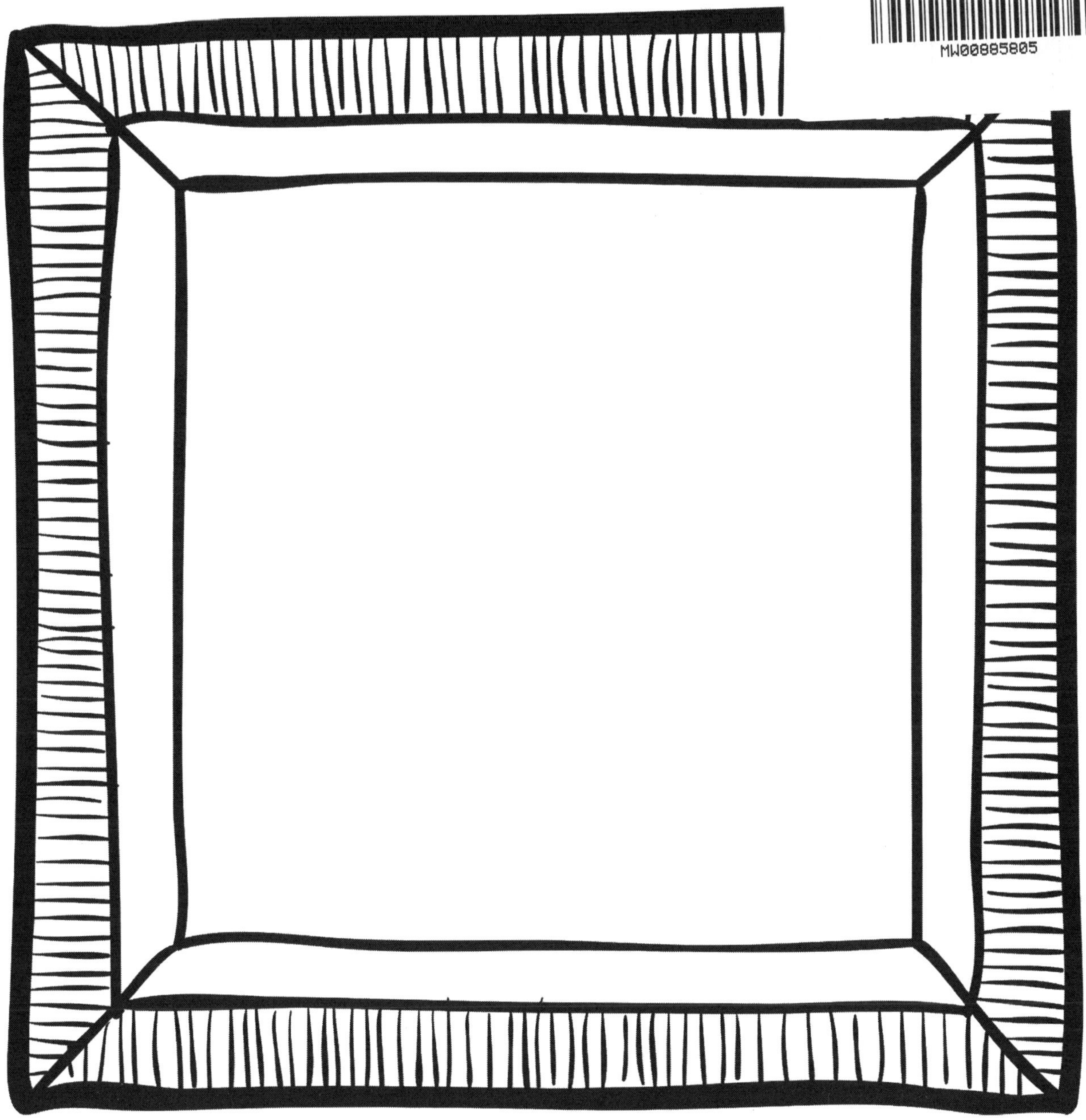

This is me!

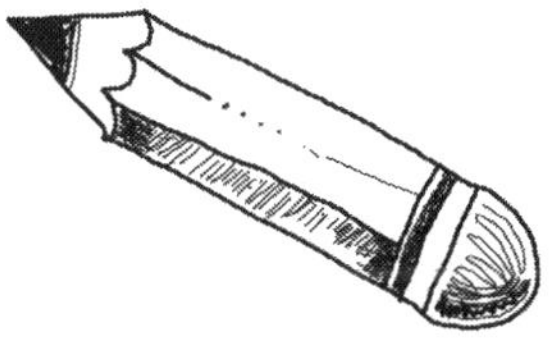

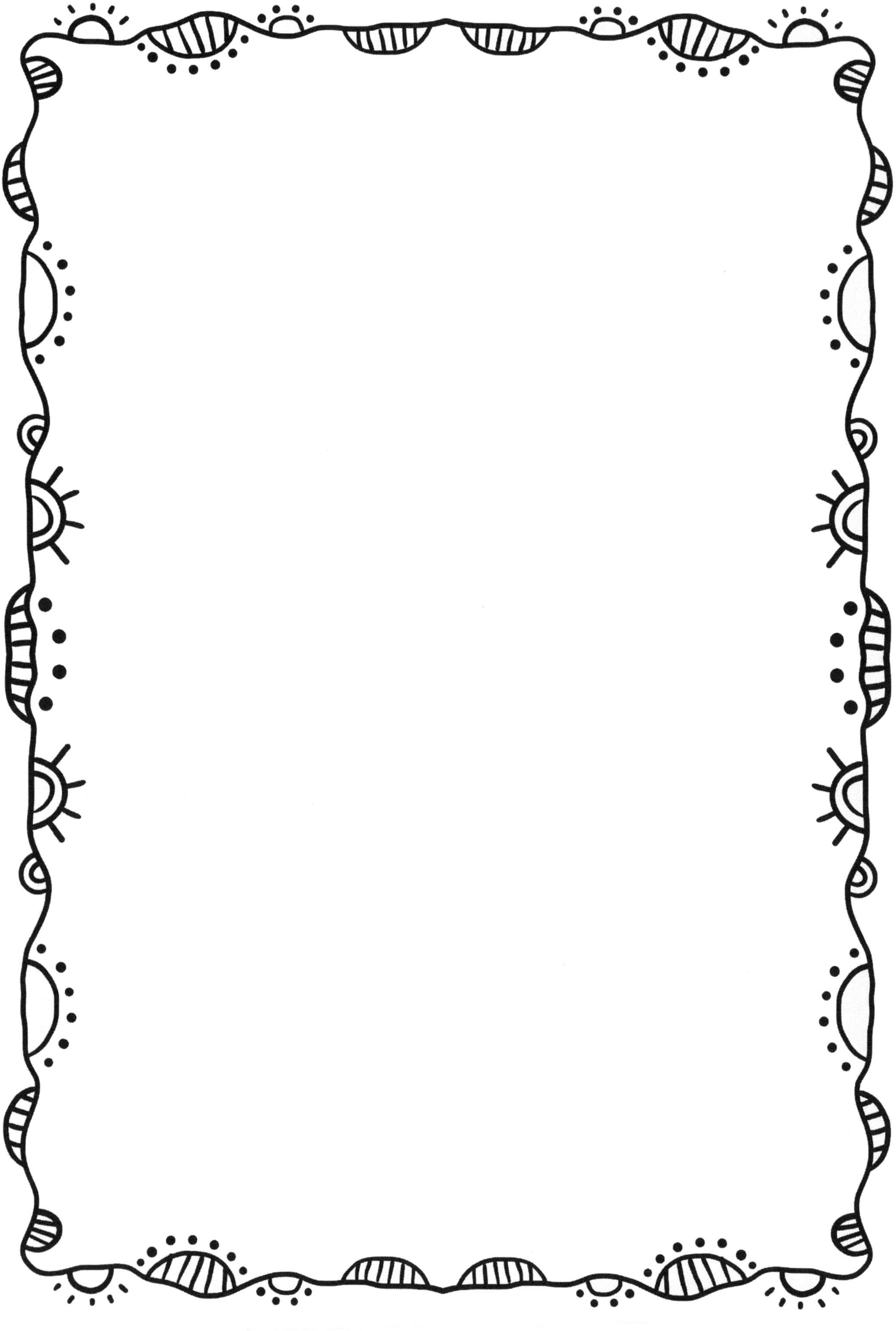

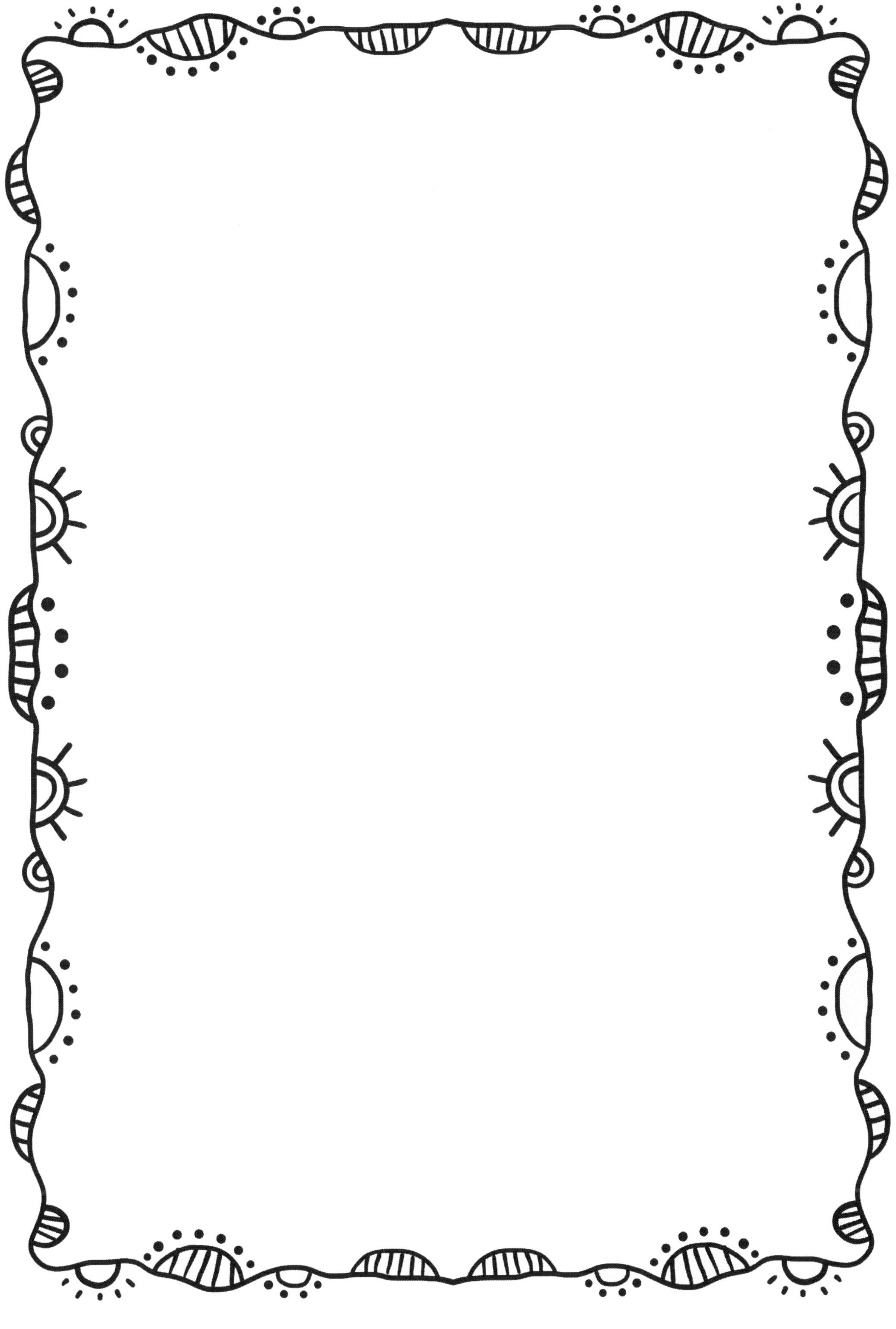

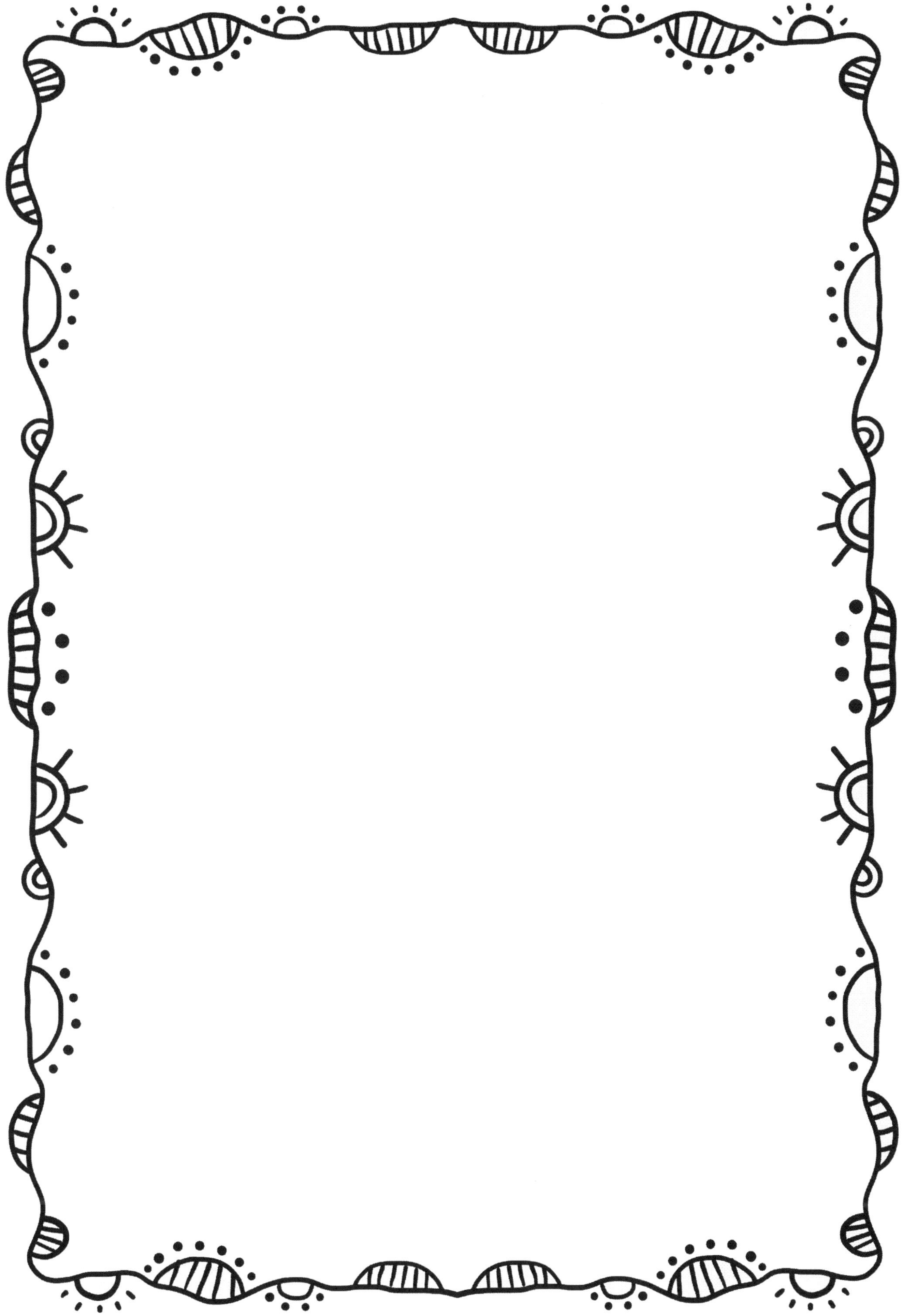

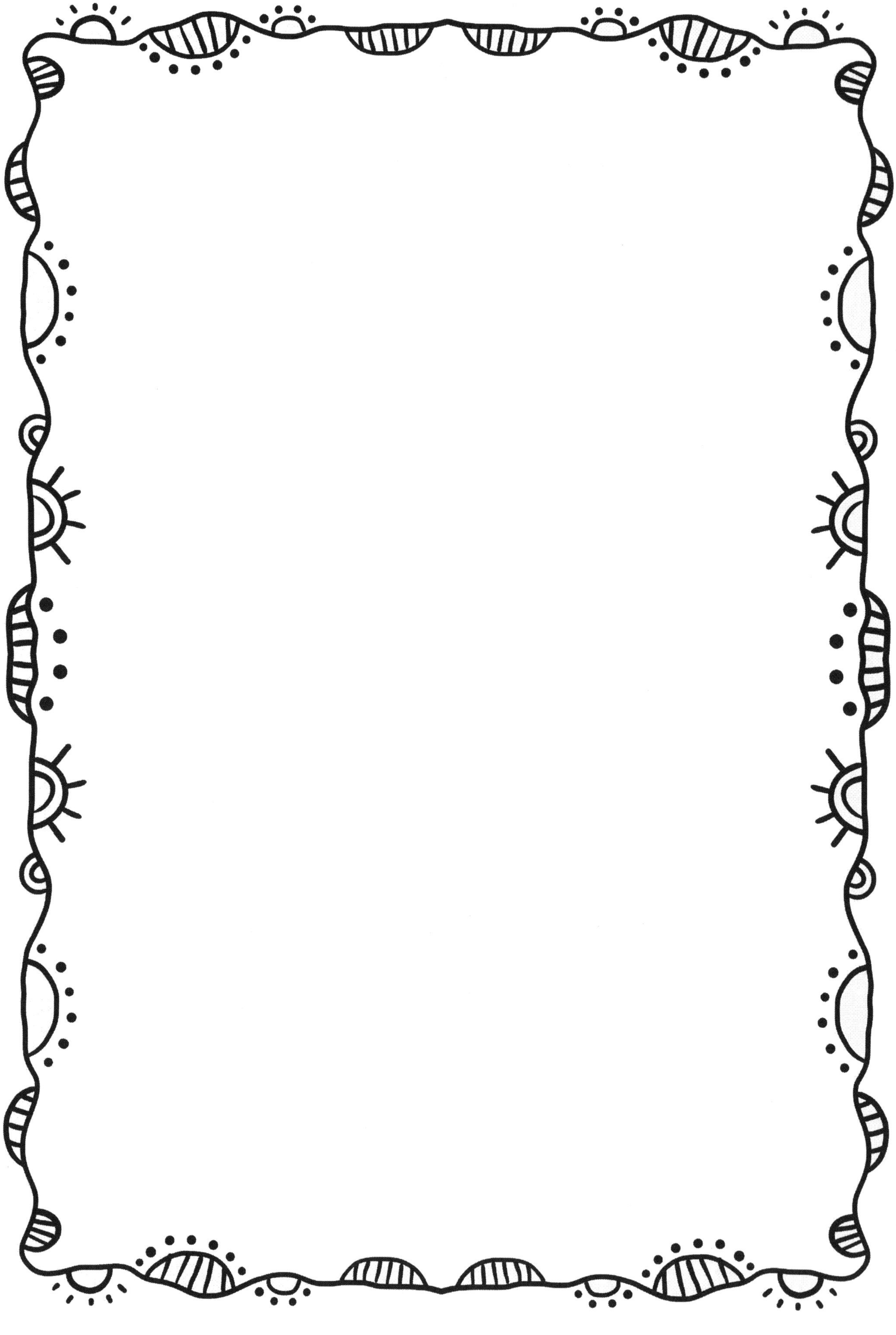

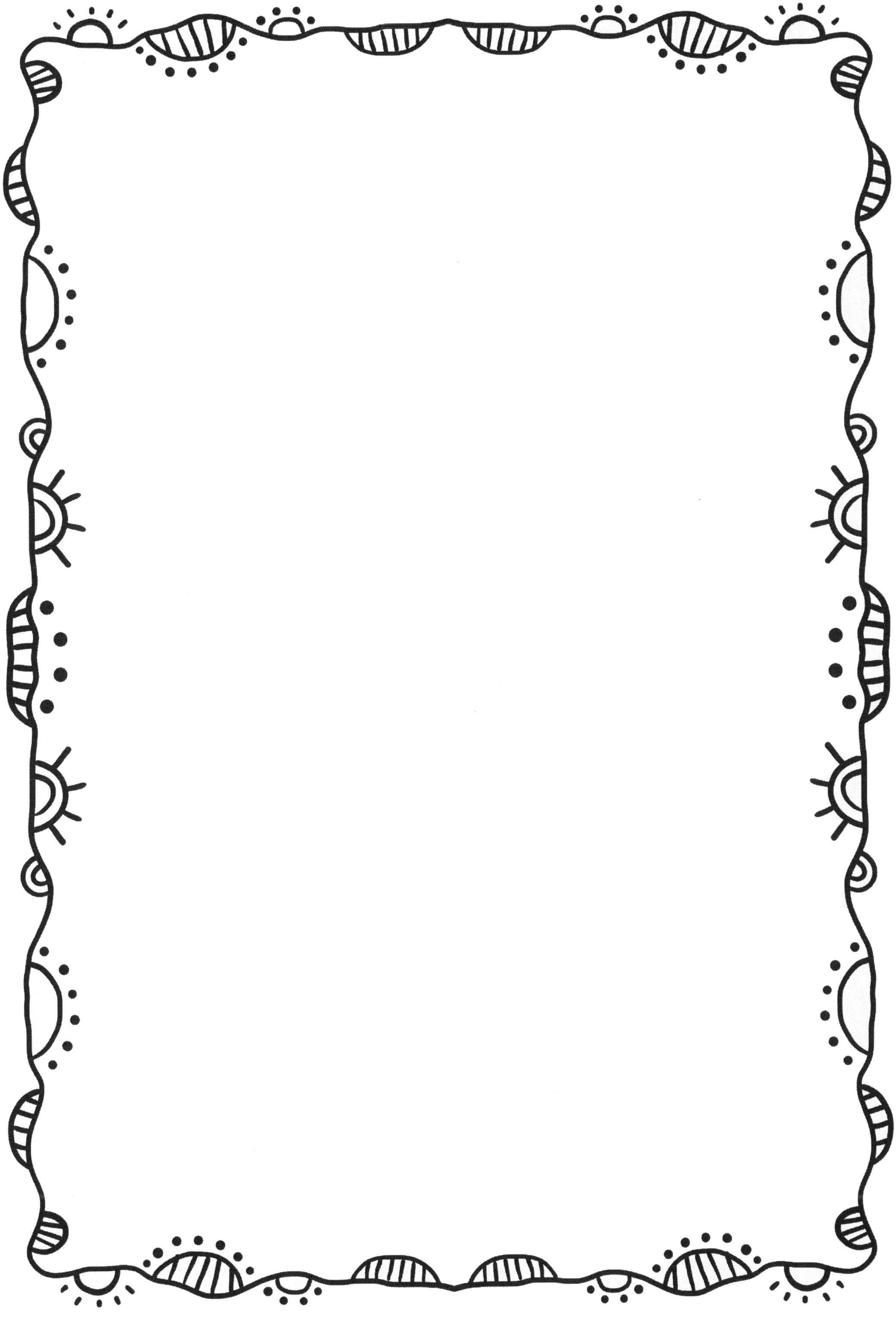

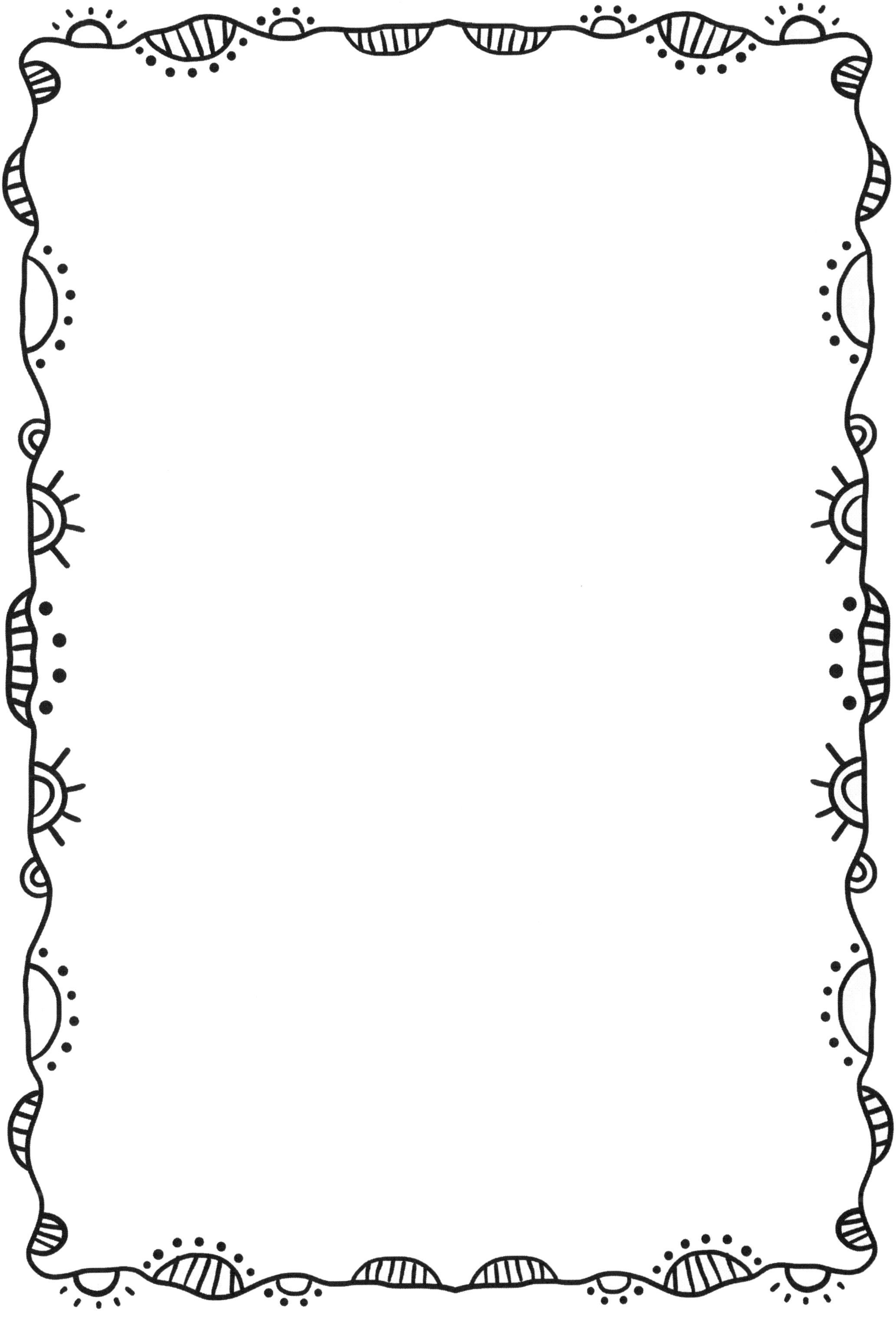

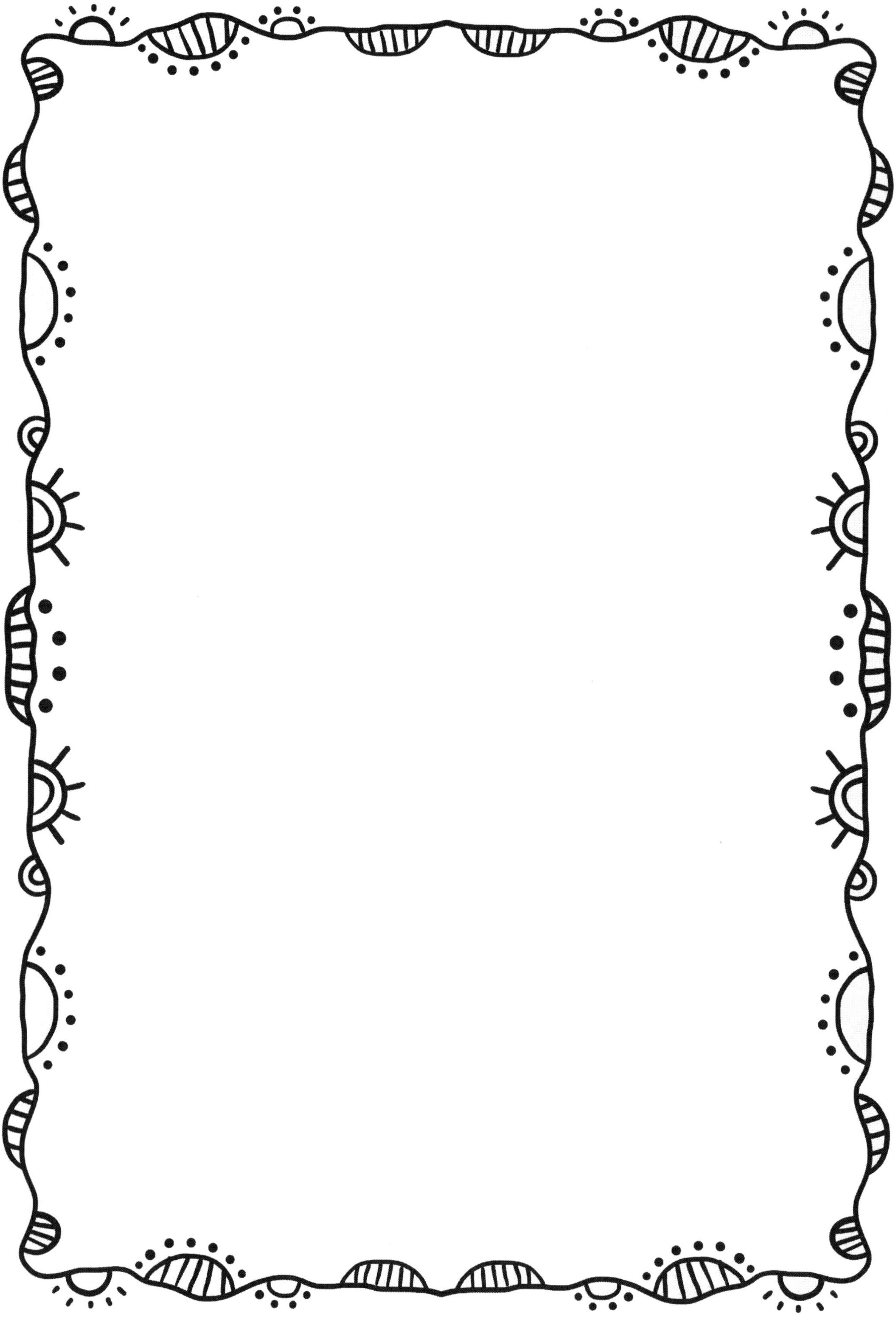

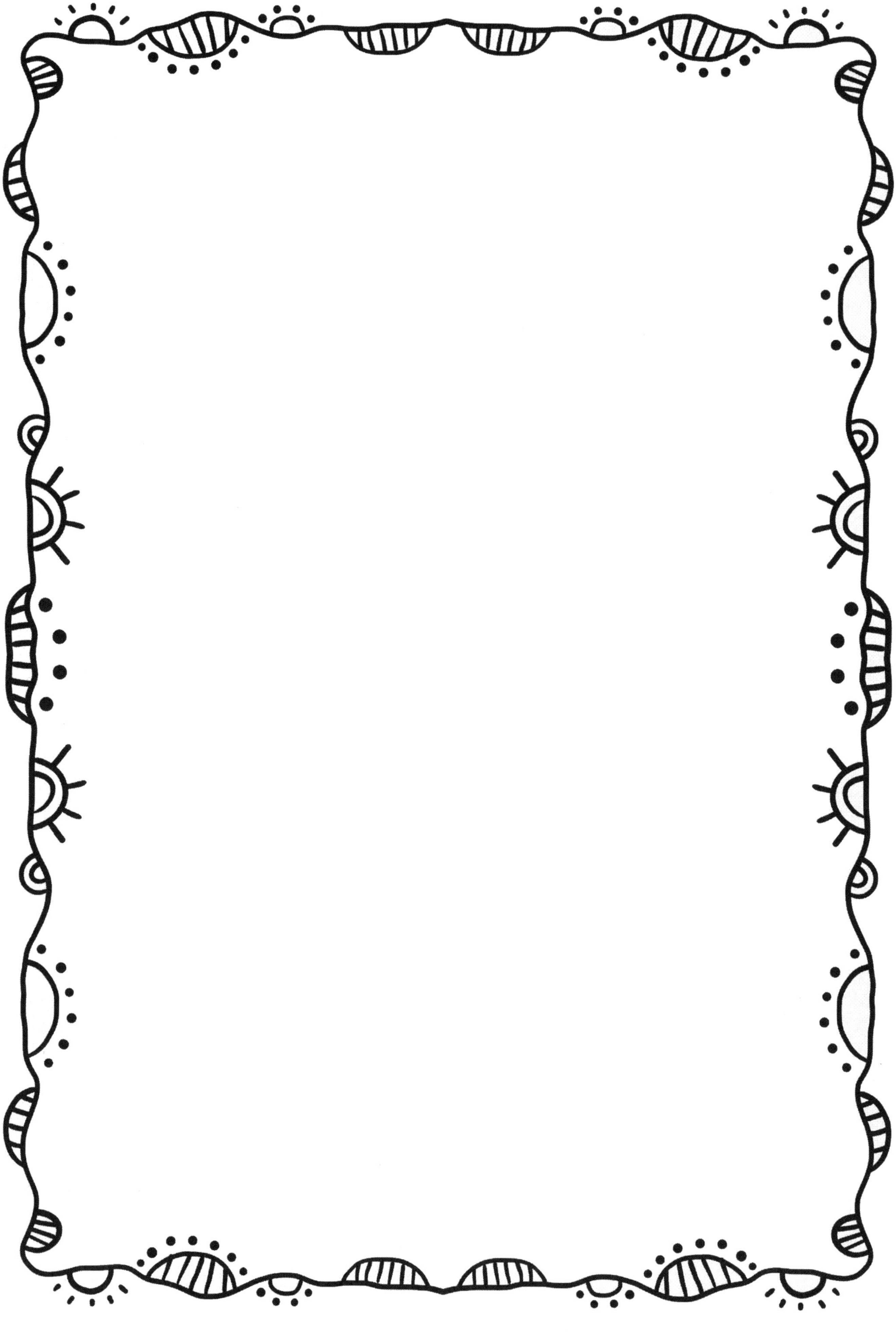

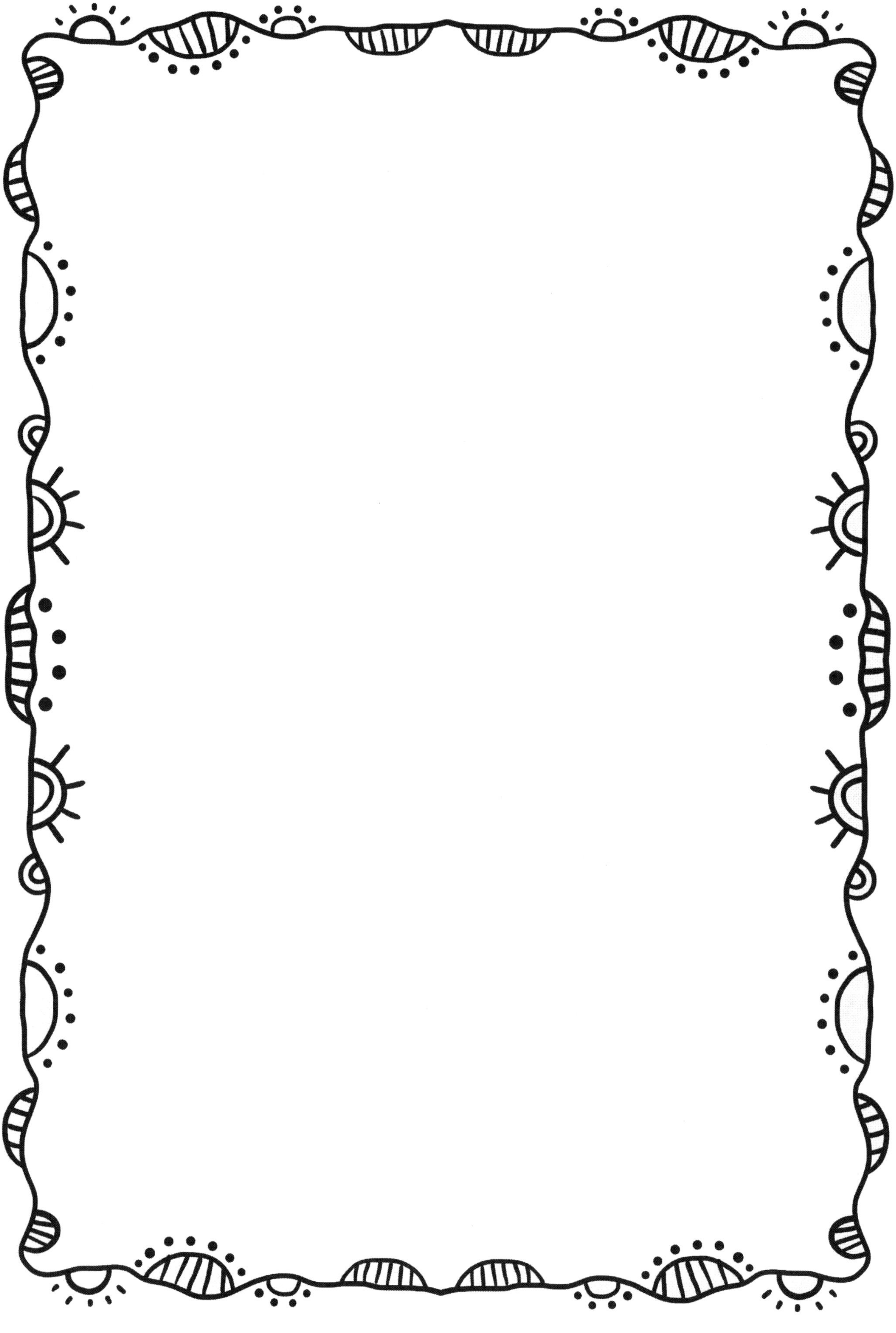

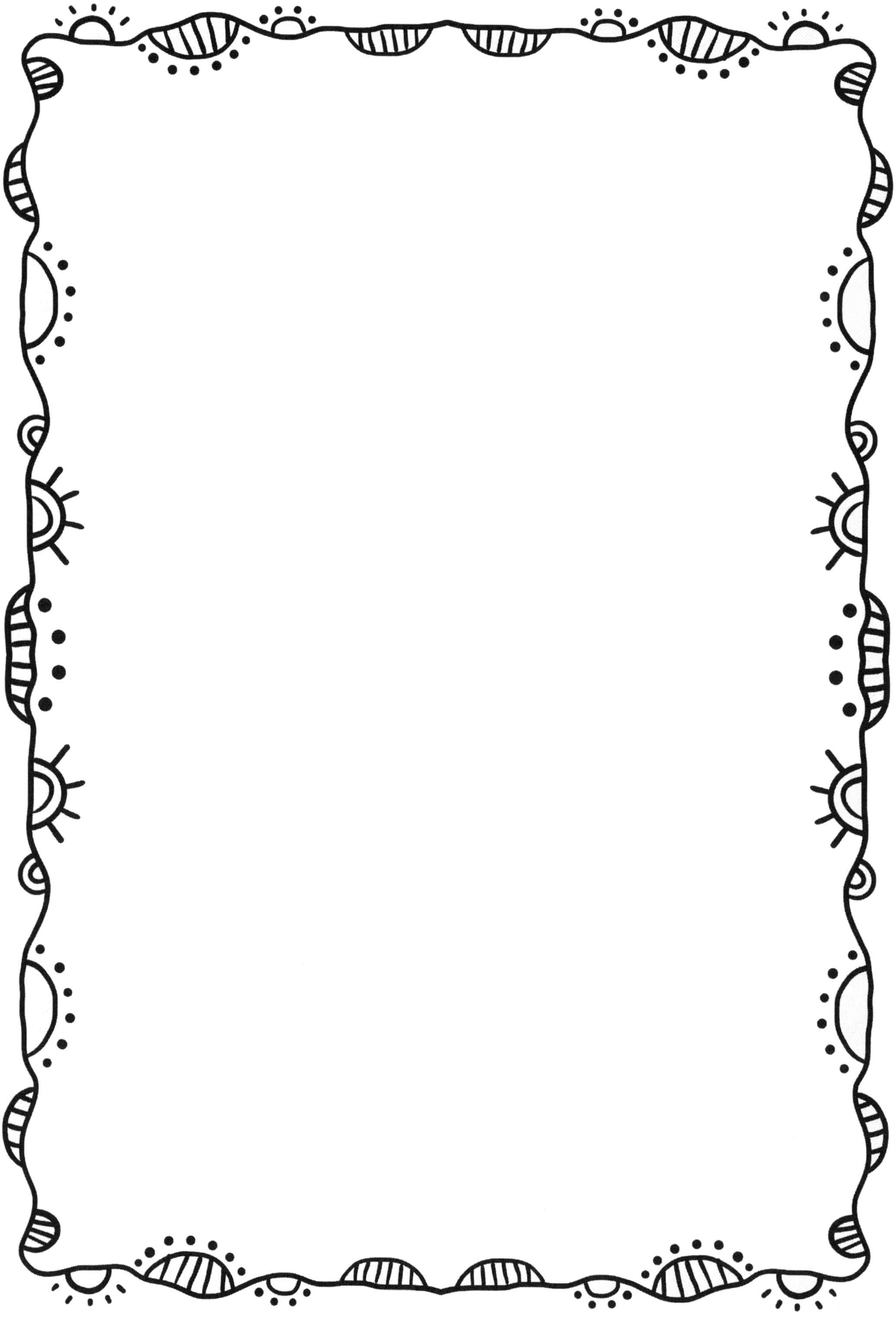

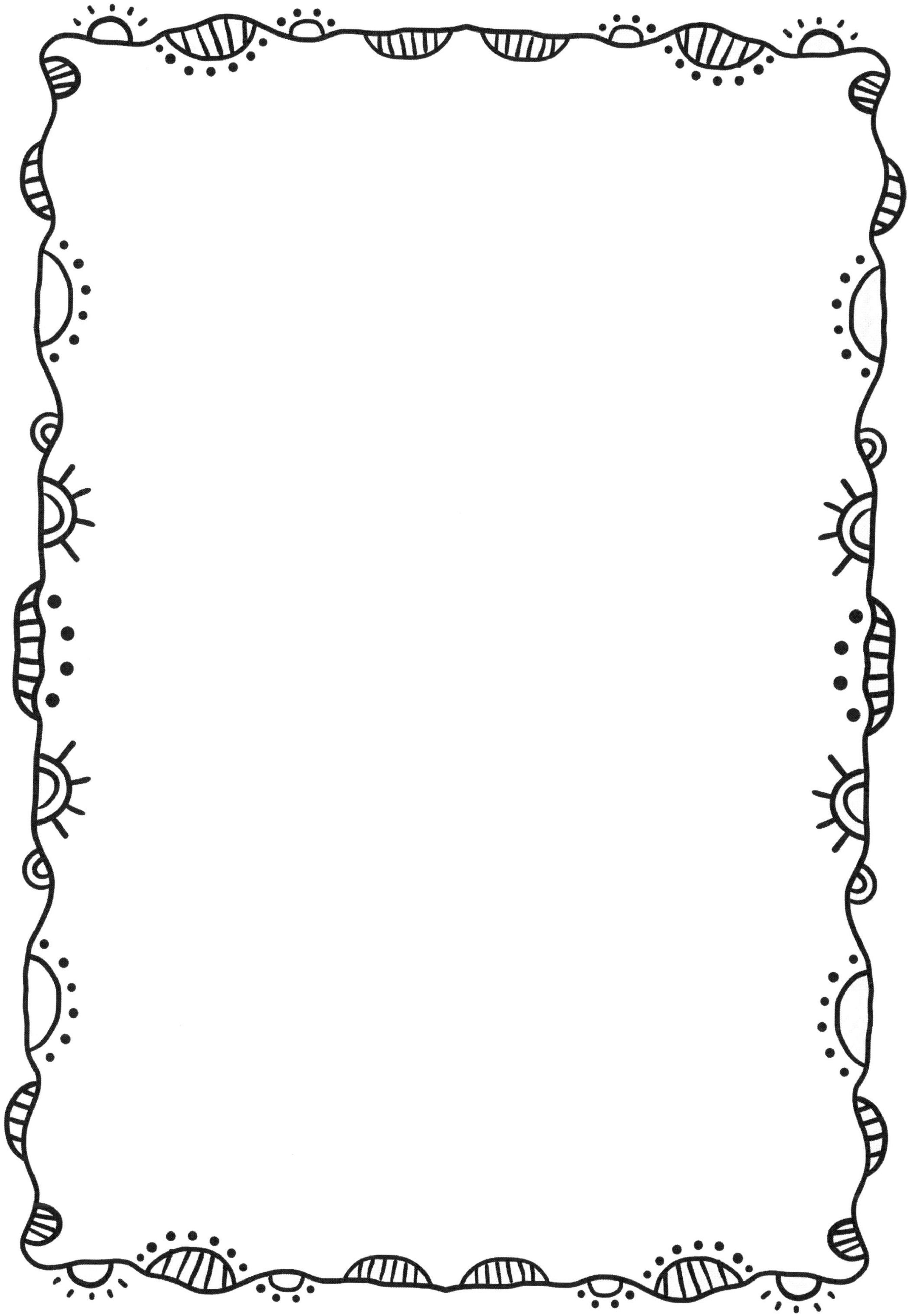

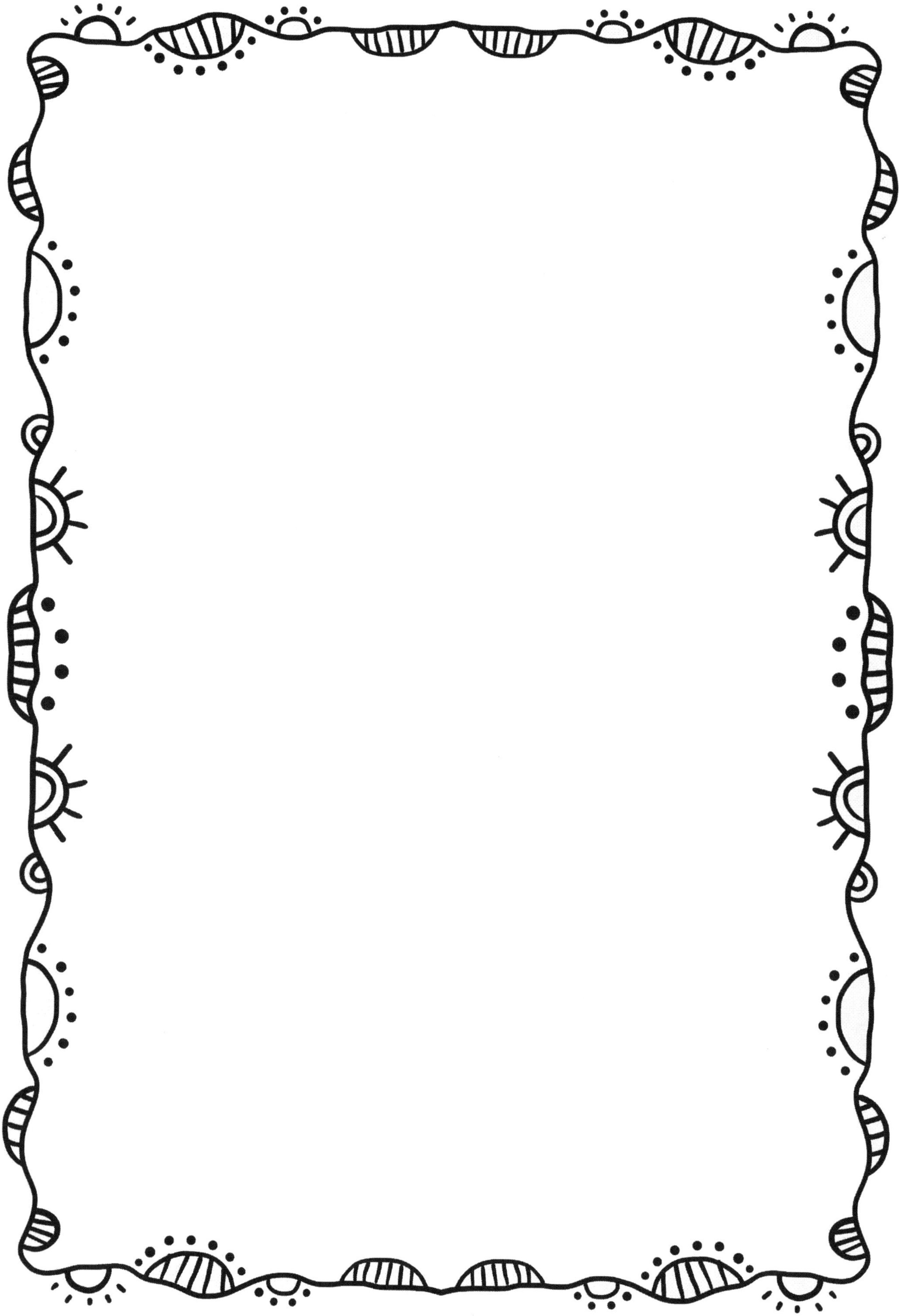

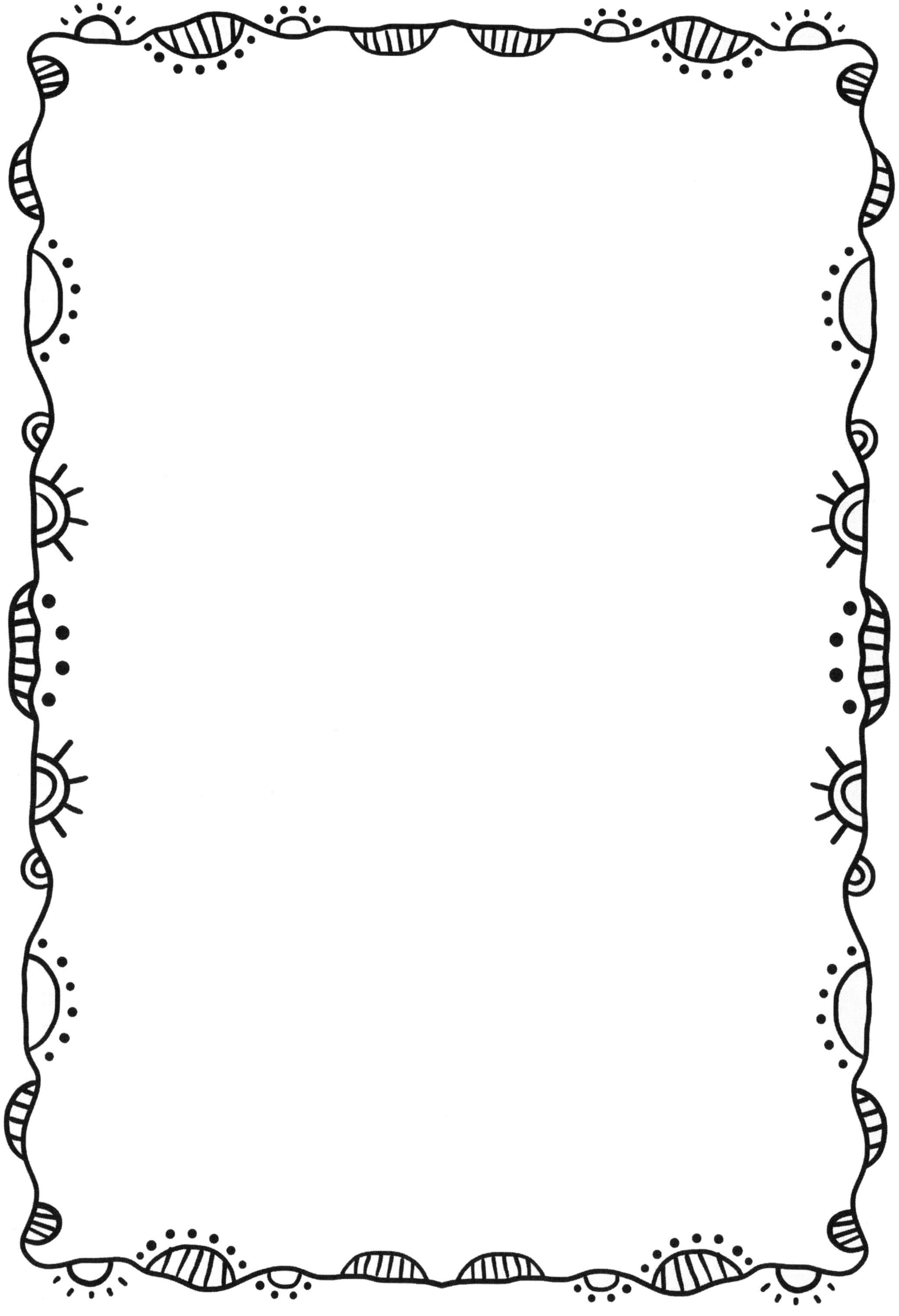

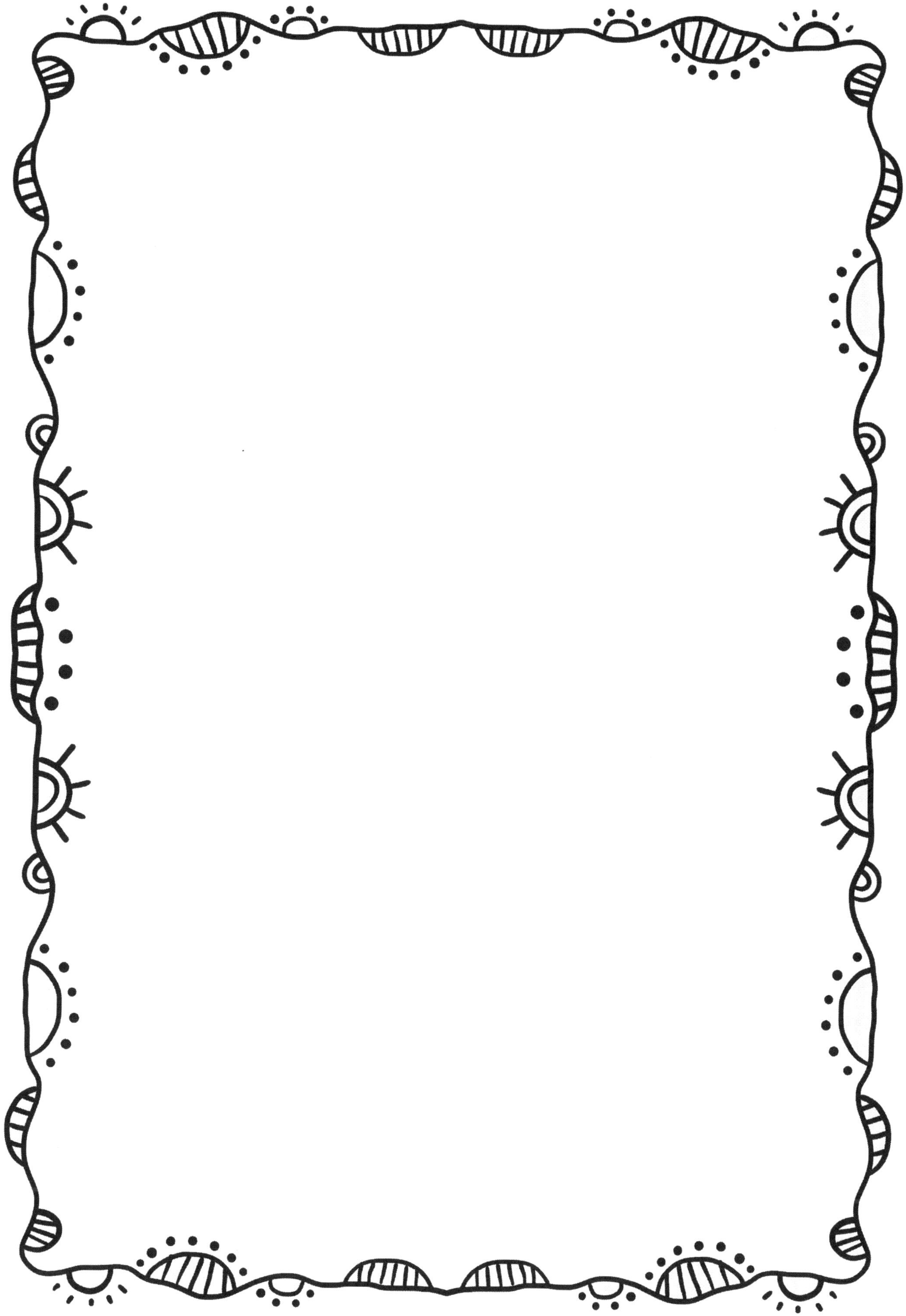

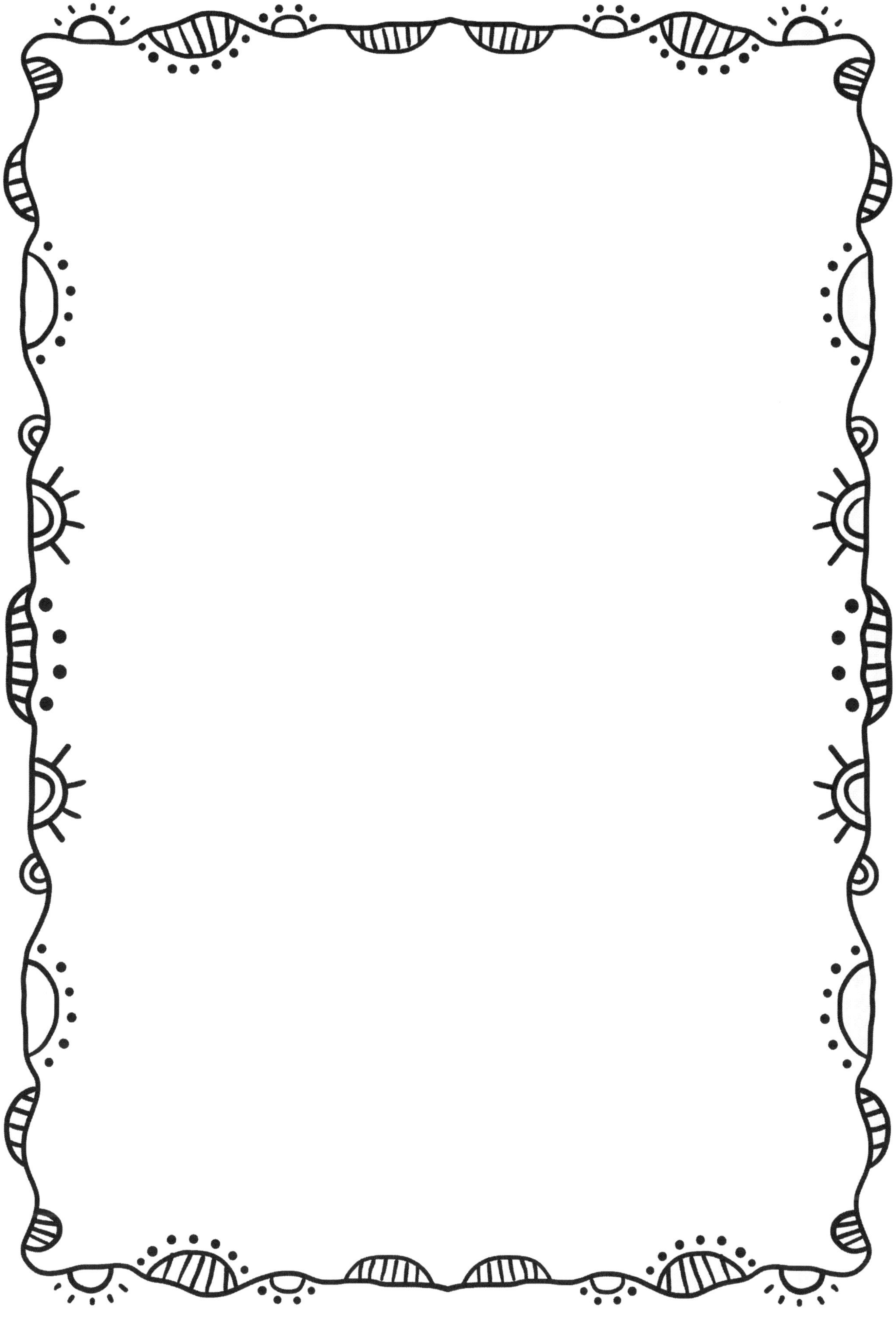

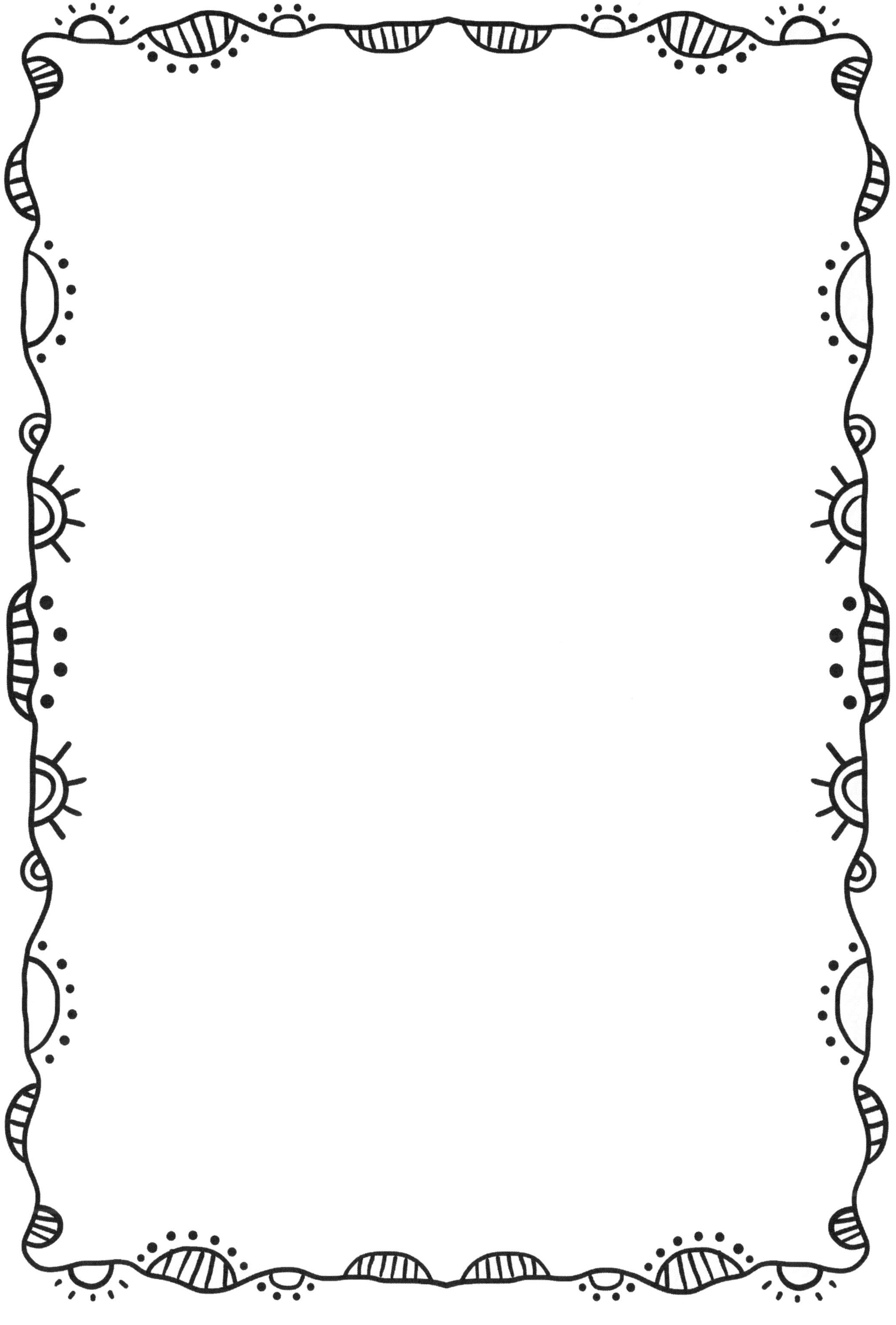

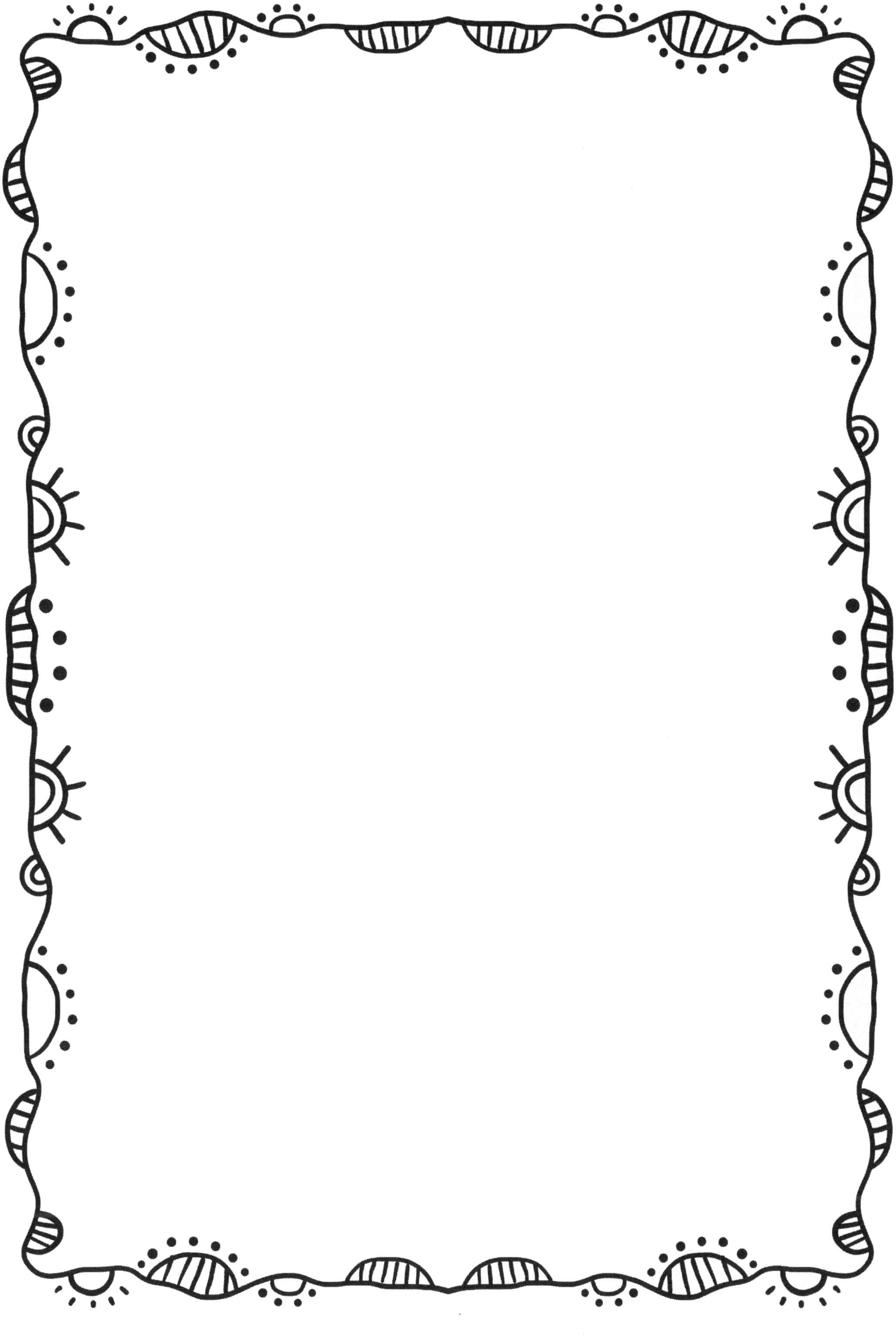

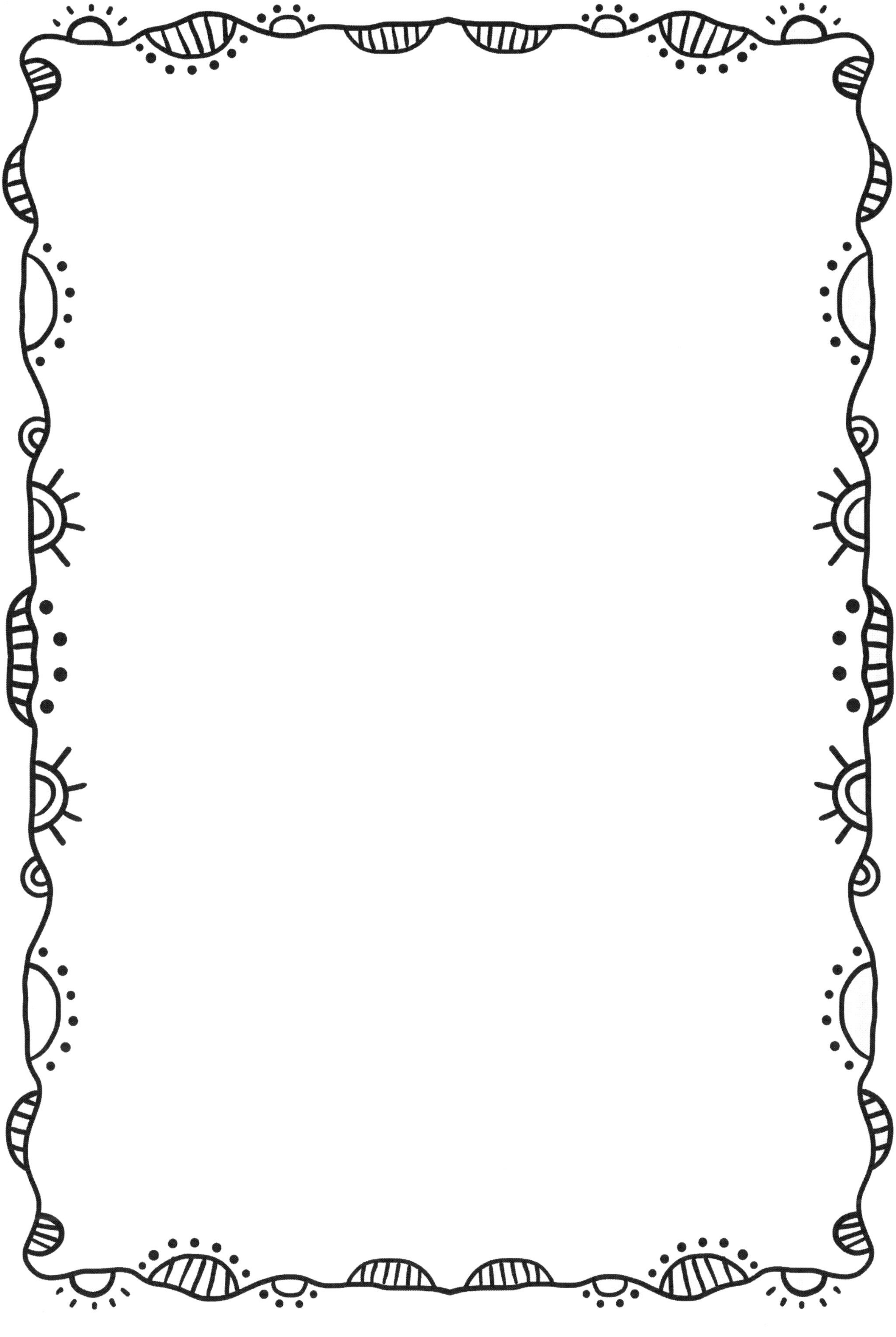

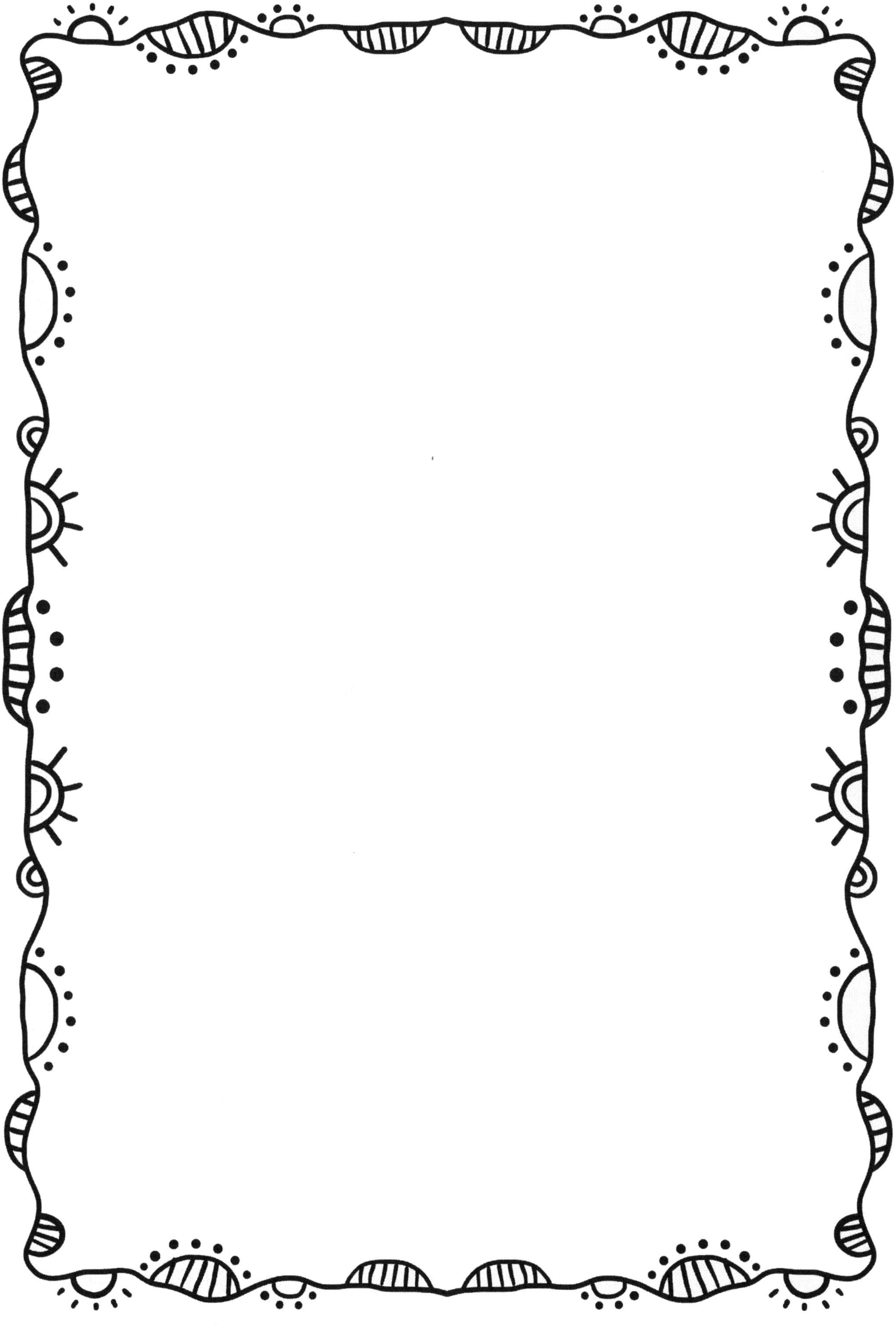

MORE THAN NOTEBOOKS kids

Made in the USA
Coppell, TX
13 February 2021

50316953R10061